How to Unlock Wealth:

Unveiling the Secrets to Financial Abundance

By

I0454575

PAUL T. KAAN

Table of contents

Introduction:

In the multifaceted embroidered artwork of life, one string winds through the texture of our encounters with significant importance—our relationship with cash. "Step-by-step instructions to Open Riches: Divulging the Key to Monetary Overflow" is an investigation into the craftsmanship and study of dominating this relationship, rising above the simple amassing of money to disentangle the privileged insights of genuine monetary overflow.

At the core of this excursion lies the acknowledgment that abundance isn't simply an objective but a dynamic and purposeful pursuit. The pages of this guide unfurl a guide, welcoming perusers to explore the scene of individual budget with reason, intelligence, and a dream for persevering through thriving.

In our current reality, where monetary decisions echo through each part of our lives, from the rooftops over our heads to the encounters we relish, defining clear monetary objectives turns into the compass for this endeavor. The presentation sets the stage by enlightening the significant significance of these objectives—more than simple numbers, they are the directing lights that shape our monetary predeterminations.

As we dive into the layers of building a strong monetary establishment, the presentation lays the foundation for grasping the meaning of trained propensities and key choices. It presents the idea of a secret stash—a monetary wellbeing net that changes unexpected difficulties from unfavourable obstacles to reasonable obstacles.

Saving arises as an incredible asset, not bound to the demonstration of gathering reserves but stretching out to the actual embodiment of developing an overflow mentality. This presentation verbalises the extraordinary idea of saving, where it turns out to be in excess of a monetary propensity—it turns into a way of thinking, a mentality that perceives the potential for development and thrives in each monetary choice.

Shrewd money management, a perplexing interaction of technique and informed independent direction, is divulged as an excursion of conceivable outcomes. The presentation lights the flash of interest, welcoming perusers to investigate the subtleties of speculation scenes, to grasp the dance of chance and prize, and to embrace a drawn-out point of view that rises above market vacillations.

Broadening systems, similar to strokes on a craftsman's material, weave a story of versatility. The presentation presents the idea of spreading risk and making a portfolio that isn't simply an assortment of ventures but a fort against the unusualness of monetary business sectors. It portrays intentional and key abundance insurance.

Remaining informed about monetary patterns arises as a signal, directing perusers through the intricacies of a globalised monetary scene. The presentation highlights the force of information, empowering perusers to explore financial flows with certainty, settle on informed choices, and quickly take advantage of chances that emerge in the midst of the back and forth movement of monetary tides.

Developing an overflow outlook turns into a key subject, welcoming perusers to rise above shortage mindsets and embrace a way of thinking of appreciation, cooperation, and faith in boundless potential outcomes. The presentation establishes the vibe for an outlook shift—a worldview that goes past monetary choices, penetrating each part of life.

Monetary propensities for progress, woven into the texture of day-to-day existence, arise as the mysterious elements for persevering through thriving. The presentation discloses the extraordinary effect of trained propensities, from planning and saving to money management shrewdly, making a story that places achievement not in stupendous motions but rather in the consistency of positive ways of behaving.

At last, as the excursion unfolds, the presentation lays the foundation for exploring difficulties. It recognises the certainty of misfortunes but presents methodologies—from building crisis assets to arranging and looking for esteem—that change difficulties into potential open doors for development. Fundamentally, the prologue to "How to Open Riches" is a greeting. It entices perusers to leave on an excursion—an excursion that rises above monetary methodologies and numbers on accounting reports. It is an excursion into the core of our relationship with cash, a journey for overflow that reverberates in our ledgers as well as in the extravagance of our lives.

Section 1

Characterising Your Monetary Objectives:

In the maze of individual accounting, clarity of direction is the compass that directs each monetary choice and shapes the direction of one's monetary excursion. "Characterising Your Monetary Objectives" isn't simply a part yet but the foundation of the whole story in "How to Open Riches: Revealing the Key to Monetary Overflow." This segment unfurls as a significant investigation into the groundbreaking influence of setting clear and deliberate monetary targets.

At its essence, characterising monetary objectives is certainly not a simple practice in numbers; it is a profoundly private and reflective excursion. The section opens with an encouragement to imagine the future, to express yearnings, and to make a guide that lines up with one's remarkable dreams and desires. It perceives that genuine abundance isn't just about gathering cash but also about directing monetary assets towards a purpose that impacts one's qualities and vision forever.

The presentation probably digs into the double idea of monetary objectives—the present moment and the long haul. Momentary objectives might incorporate putting something aside for a get-away, buying another contraption, or building a backup stash. They are the venturing stones that give a feeling of achievement and substantial advancement. Then again, long-haul objectives are the fantastic ensemble of one's monetary arrangement, like purchasing a home, subsidising training, or resigning serenely. Together, they structure an agreeable system that outlines the course of a satisfying monetary life.

Reasonable guidance on distinguishing and articulating these objectives is a critical component of this section. The writer might acquaint activities or systems with assistance perusers unwind their monetary yearnings. This includes a course of contemplation, posing inquiries that go past money-related values to dig into the pith of a significant life. What encounters would you like to have? What values drive your monetary choices? What inheritance do you seek to leave?

An investigation into the mental aspects of an objective setting is possible in this part. The force of representation, confirmations, and the profound association with monetary objectives are disclosed as devices that rise above the domain of calculation sheets and numbers. The part recognises that monetary objectives are not static; they advance as life unfolds. Subsequently, developing an adaptable outlook turns into a key component, empowering people to adjust their objectives to changing conditions without failing to focus on their general vision.

The account may likewise address the job of monetary objectives in providing inspiration and motivation. A clear-cut objective isn't simply a far-off target; a wellspring of motivation impacts everyday monetary choices. Whether it's opposing the enticement of a drive-buy or remaining trained in saving, the arrangement, with a reasonable reason, pushes people forward on their monetary excursion.

The prologue to "Characterising Your Monetary Objectives" makes way for the reasonable parts that follow. It is the establishment whereupon the whole book rests—an establishment based on the conviction that monetary overflow is definitely not an irregular result but rather a conscious pursuit. By characterising their monetary objectives, perusers leave on an excursion that rises above the intricacies of individual budgets, changing their relationship with cash into a deliberate and purposeful journey for persevering through riches and satisfaction.

Building a strong monetary establishment is fundamental for long-term monetary achievement. This includes making a financial plan, overseeing costs, and laying out a secret stash. A solid groundwork gives security and versatility, empowering people to seek after their monetary objectives.
with certainty.

Section 2

Building a Strong Monetary Establishment:

In the ensemble of individual accounting, the idea of building a strong monetary establishment reverberates as the essential note—the harmony that sets the musicality for an amicable and versatile monetary life. The section "Building a Strong Monetary Establishment" in "How to Open Riches: Disclosing the Key to Monetary Overflow" unfurls as an exhaustive aide, digging into the mind-boggling parts that develop this fundamental basis.

The section starts with a piercing affirmation—a comprehension that genuine monetary achievement isn't just about procuring more; it's tied in with enhancing the utilisation of what one has. The initial segment probably highlights the significance of an outlook shift—an enlivening of the extraordinary capability of trained monetary propensities and deliberate independent direction.

At its centre, constructing a strong monetary establishment is a dynamic and continuous interaction. It includes a diverse methodology that tends to different features of an individual budget. The part probably unfurls into the accompanying key parts:

1. Planning as the Foundation:

The idea of planning is presented as the foundation of monetary soundness. Planning isn't just about confining spending; it is an essential distribution of assets, a guide that directs each monetary choice. The section gives useful insights into making a financial plan that lines up with individual objectives, stressing the meaning of following and dissecting costs.

2. Trained Cost Administration:

The story investigates the craft of trained cost administration—a cognizant work to recognise needs and needs. It urges perusers to focus on fundamental uses while controlling pointless spending. The section probably gives functional tips on developing careful ways of managing money and settling on informed decisions that line up with long-term monetary goals.

3. Laying out a secret stash:
A critical support point in building monetary strength is the foundation of a backup stash. The part jumps into the significance of having a monetary wellbeing net—an asset that pads against unforeseen costs or pay interruptions. Functional exhortations on deciding the proper size of the backup stash and systems for steady commitments are logically tended to.

4. Obligation The board systems:
The section unfurls into the domain of obligation on the board; it is impeding the recognition that not all obligations Key utilisation of obligation, for example, for speculation or instruction, is examined closely by judicious obligation decrease systems. The story explores the subtleties of recognising "great" and "awful" obligations and gives experiences into limiting exorbitant interest obligations.

5. Living Inside Means:
Building a strong monetary establishment is inseparable from living within one's means. The part investigates the brain science behind this propensity, underscoring the extraordinary force of adjusting the way of life to pay. It urges perusers to oppose the charm of way-of-life expansion and embrace an economical and adjusted way to deal with spending.

6. Constant Improvement and Learning:
The excursion to monetary solidity is portrayed by ceaseless improvement and learning. The part presents the idea of monetary schooling, asking perusers to remain informed about individual accounting standards, speculation systems, and financial patterns. It stresses the strengthening that comes with information and the capacity to settle on informed monetary choices.

7. Long-haul Vision and Objective Arrangement:
The idea of building a strong monetary establishment reaches beyond quick requirements. The part probably prompts perusers to interface their monetary propensities with long-haul dreams and objectives. It investigates the transaction between momentary activities and the general monetary story, empowering people to adjust their everyday choices to their more extensive monetary desires.

The prologue to "Building a Strong Monetary Establishment" isn't simply a manual for overseeing cash; it is a challenge to develop monetary strength, soundness, and strengthening. It makes way for ensuing sections, where perusers will dig further into every part, obtaining the devices and bits of knowledge to build an establishment that endures the everyday hardships and prepares for persevering through monetary achievement.

Section 3

The Force of Saving:

Setting aside cash isn't simply a monetary propensity; an incredible asset can shape one's monetary future and cultivate a conviction that all is good and freedom. The demonstration of saving includes saving a part of pay routinely, and its effect stretches out a long way past collecting reserves. It shapes the foundation of monetary prosperity, impacting different parts of an individual's budget.

One of the critical parts of the force of saving lies in its capacity to make a monetary pad. By reliably saving a level of pay, people fabricate a secret stash, giving a security net to unanticipated conditions. This asset fills in as monetary support during startling occasions, like health-related crises or unexpected employment cutbacks, offering genuine serenity and relieving the effect of monetary shocks.

Saving likewise works with objective accomplishment. Whether the goal is purchasing a home, beginning a business, or financing training, the propensity for saving changes yearnings into unmistakable, feasible targets. Standard commitments to bank accounts or venture portfolios aggregate over the long run, intensifying the development of assets and carrying people closer to their monetary objectives.

Besides, saving imparts monetary discipline. It requires a promise to postpone delight and a cognizant effort to focus on long-term monetary prosperity over prompt cravings. This discipline stretches beyond the demonstration of saving itself, impacting ways of managing money and empowering insightful monetary direction.

The force of saving is additionally intensified by the idea of accumulating funds. As reserve funds create returns, these profits, thus, contribute to the general development of the investment funds. Over the long haul, the intensifying impact can altogether improve the worth of saved reserves, turning little, reliable commitments into significant monetary resources.

Moreover, saving gives an establishment to speculation. The assets collected through saving can be decisively contributed to create unexpected returns. This presents the potential for abundance creation and monetary thriving beyond what saving alone can accomplish.

Taking everything into account, the influence of saving extends beyond the collection of cash. It encourages monetary versatility, upholds objective accomplishment, ingrains discipline, uses the advantages of progressive accrual, and sets out open doors for speculation. Embracing the propensity for saving isn't simply a monetary choice; it is an extraordinary move towards building a protected and prosperous monetary future.

Section 4

Contributing Carefully:

Contributing shrewdly is a key and dynamic cycle that goes beyond simply designating reserves; it is an insightful excursion towards abundance collection and monetary development. The demonstration of financial planning includes sending capital with the assumption of creating returns, and the standards of shrewd putting are grounded in a blend of exploration, risk-taking, and a drawn-out viewpoint.

At the centre of effective financial planning is the significance of informed navigation. This starts with an exhaustive comprehension of one's monetary objectives, risk resilience, and time skyline. By adjusting speculations to these key variables, people can fit their portfolios to meet their extraordinary targets. Savvy financial backers perceive that every speculation ought to fill a particular need within the more extensive setting of their monetary arrangement.

Enhancement is a vital principle of insightful financial planning. Spreading ventures across various resource classes, like stocks, bonds, and land, mitigates risk. An expanded portfolio is less defenceless to the variances of any single market or industry, laying the groundwork for long-term development.

Risk management is a fundamental part of financial planning. While better yields frequently go with higher dangers, a judicious financial backer surveys and balances risk factors. This includes grasping the instability of various resources, remaining informed about market drifts, and carrying out risk moderation methodologies, for example, setting stop-misfortune arrangements or enhancing across areas.

The significance of a drawn-out point of view couldn't possibly be more significant in savvy, effective money management. Markets might encounter transient changes, yet a patient methodology permits financial backers to brave unpredictability and advantage from the compounding of profits after some time. Shrewd financial backers oppose the enticement of responding hastily to showcase changes and spotlight the general direction of their speculations.

Persistent learning is one more sign of insightful financial planning. Monetary business sectors advance, and remaining informed about financial patterns, industry improvements, and worldwide events is significant. Savvy financial backers commit time to progressing schooling, utilising assets, and looking for guidance to pursue informed choices in a consistently changing monetary scene.

All in all, contributing shrewdly is a nuanced and dynamic cycle that includes informed direction, expansion, risk-taking, a drawn-out point of view, and persistent learning. By embracing these standards, financial backers position themselves not exclusively to explore the intricacies of monetary business sectors but additionally to saddle the potential for manageable and significant abundance aggregation over the long haul.

Section 5
Broadening Techniques:

Broadening is a key rule in speculation that implies spreading risk across a range of resources to improve the general security and execution of a portfolio. The idea perceives that various sorts of speculations might respond distinctively to different economic situations, and by joining them decisively, financial backers mean to lessen the effect of poor-performing resources on the general portfolio. Expansion techniques are indispensable to building a versatile venture portfolio, and they include a few key standards.

One of the essential broadening techniques includes distributing speculation across various resource classes. This regularly incorporates a blend of values (stocks), fixed-pay protections (securities), and elective ventures (like land or wares). Every resource class responds distinctively to monetary circumstances; for example, stocks might offer exceptional yields but accompany higher instability, while securities furnish strength yet have possibly lower returns. The right equilibrium relies upon the financial backer's gamble resistance, monetary objectives, and time skyline.

Inside every resource class, geographic broadening is another critical methodology. By putting resources into different locales and nations, financial backers can decrease their openness to country-explicit dangers and benefit from worldwide monetary development. This approach helps defend the portfolio from unfriendly occasions that might influence a specific district, like financial slumps or international vulnerabilities.

Area broadening is one more methodology that includes spreading speculation across various enterprises or areas of the economy. Ventures can be repeated, with shifting execution in view of financial circumstances. By enhancing across areas, financial backers can moderate the gamble related to the underperformance of a particular industry.

Besides, enhancement reaches out to individual protections inside every resource class. As opposed to investing vigorously in a couple of individual stocks or bonds, a very differentiated portfolio incorporates an expansive scope of property. This approach lessens the effect of poor-performing individual ventures and improves the potential for general portfolio soundness.

In the domain of elective ventures, methodologies like putting resources into land, items, or confidential value can add an additional layer of broadening. These resources frequently have a low connection with customary stocks and securities, providing a fence against market instability.

While broadening is a strong gamble for the executives device, it's vital to note that it doesn't ensure benefits or kill every likely gamble. In any case, it remains a foundation of reasonable speculation, assisting financial backers with exploring the intricacies of monetary business sectors and constructing portfolios that are stronger than the flighty idea of the venture scene. By embracing enhanced procedures, financial backers position themselves to more readily weather conditions and market vacillations and seek out additional steady, long-term returns.

Section 6

Remaining Informed about Monetary Patterns:

In the powerful scene of monetary business sectors, remaining informed about financial patterns is a basic practice for financial backers and people alike. Financial patterns have a significant impact on different parts of an individual's budget, from venture choices to business possibilities. By effectively observing and understanding these patterns, people can settle on informed choices that line up with more extensive monetary circumstances, adding to monetary soundness and development.

One of the critical motivations to remain informed about financial patterns is to expect and answer shifts in the business cycle. Monetary cycles, portrayed by times of extension, constriction, and recuperation, influence speculation returns, business potential, and expansion rates. By perceiving the ongoing period of the monetary cycle, people can change their monetary techniques appropriately. For example, during monetary developments, financial backers should seriously mull over a more forceful venture approach, while in times of compression, a more safe position could be reasonable.

Expansion is one more pivotal financial point to screen. Expansion disintegrates the buying influence of cash after some time, influencing the genuine worth of reserve funds and speculations. Remaining informed about expansion patterns empowers people to make changes in accordance with their speculation portfolios and monetary designs to neutralise the expected effect of rising costs.

Financing costs, set by national banks, assume an essential role in monetary elements. Changes in loan fees impact acquiring costs, speculation returns, and buyer spending. Staying up-to-date with financing cost patterns assists people in arriving at informed conclusions about advances, home loans, and speculation procedures. For instance, in an increasing financing cost climate, people could rethink their plans and consider fixed-rate credits.

Worldwide monetary patterns are progressively interconnected. In a time of globalisation, occasions in a single region of the planet can have expanding influences worldwide. Checking worldwide financial patterns is fundamental for financial backers with an enhanced portfolio, and organisations take part in worldwide business sectors. Figuring out international occasions, exchange elements, and cash developments gives significant bits of knowledge to exploring the intricacies of a globalised economy.

Innovative headways have likewise changed how financial data is gotten to and dissected. Continuous information, financial pointers, and market examinations are promptly accessible, engaging people to make opportune and informed choices. Using these assets, people can remain in front of monetary patterns and proactively change their monetary plans.

All in all, remaining informed about monetary patterns is a proactive and engaging practice in the domain of individual accounting. By observing key financial markers, understanding the business cycle, and keeping up to date with worldwide turns of events, people can settle on informed choices that line up with the always-changing monetary scene. This upgrades monetary flexibility as well as positions people to gain from potential open doors and explore difficulties actually in an undeniably unique financial climate.

Section 7

Developing an Overflow Mentality:

Developing an overflow outlook is a groundbreaking way to deal with life and an individual budget that rises above simple monetary achievement. Established in certain brain research, this mentality includes encouraging a conviction that valuable open doors are boundless, achievement is feasible, and there is enough for everybody. It is a strong change in outlook that impacts monetary choices as well as one's general way to deal with difficulties, connections, and self-improvement.

At its centre, an overflow outlook challenges the shortage mindset—the conviction that assets, open doors, and achievement are restricted. Rather than survey life from a perspective of need, people with an overflow mentality see prospects and expectations in each circumstance. This change in context can have significant ramifications for monetary prosperity.

One of the vital parts of developing an overflow outlook is appreciation. Rehearsing appreciation includes valuing what one has, recognising achievements, and zeroing in on the positive parts of life. By perceiving and offering thanks for monetary victories, regardless of how little, people can encourage a feeling of overflow and draw in additional good results.

Risk-taking is one more component interwoven with an overflow attitude. People with this outlook view difficulties as open doors for development instead of impossible obstructions. This eagerness to proceed with potentially dangerous courses of action can prompt enterprising endeavours, ventures, and vocation moves that add to monetary achievement.

Besides, coordinated effort and a readiness to share achievements characterise the overflow mentality. Rather than seeing others as contenders, people with this mentality commend the accomplishments of others and perceive that achievement is certainly not a losing situation. This cooperative methodology can prompt significant organisations, organising potential open doors, and a steady local area that contributes to overall achievement.

An overflow mentality additionally accentuates constant learning and improvement. Rather than dreading disappointment, people with this mentality embrace it as a stepping stone to development. Gaining from mistakes, adjusting to difficulties, and keeping an oddity about new open doors are basic qualities of those with an overflow outlook.

In the domain of individual budgets, developing an overflow outlook impacts ways of managing money and venture choices. It urges people to see cash as a limited asset as well as an instrument for setting out open doors, encounters, and positive effects. This outlook advances a mindful monetary way of behaving while at the same time permitting people to seek after their objectives with certainty and hopefulness.

All in all, developing an overflow mentality is an all-encompassing methodology that stretches beyond monetary issues. It includes taking on an inspirational perspective on life, embracing difficulties, and cultivating a feeling of appreciation and coordinated effort. By incorporating these standards into one's mentality, people can open their maximum capacity, explore monetary choices with certainty, and eventually make a day-to-day existence wealthy in importance and
satisfaction.

Section 8

Monetary Propensities for Progress:

Progress in individual accounting isn't exclusively the aftereffect of major monetary choices yet is many times formed by everyday propensities and ways of behaving. Monetary propensities assume a urgent part in building a strong starting point for progress, adding to long haul solidness, and encouraging a sound connection with cash. The following are a few key monetary propensities that can prepare for monetary achievement:

1. Planning and Following Costs:

A major monetary propensity is making and adhering to a spending plan. Planning includes designating pay to different costs, reserve funds, and speculations. Consistently following costs guarantees familiarity with spending examples and distinguishes regions for likely reserve funds. This propensity engages people to live inside their means and designate assets productively.

2. Saving Reliably:

Saving is a foundation of monetary achievement. Developing a propensity for steady saving, whether through robotized moves to an investment account or business supported retirement plans, fabricates a monetary pad. Crisis investment funds give a security net to startling costs, while long haul investment funds add to accomplishing monetary objectives.

3. Living Beneath Means:

Effective monetary people frequently focus on living beneath their means. This includes settling on purposeful decisions to keep away from superfluous obligation and luxurious spending. By keeping a hole among pay and costs, people can gather reserve funds, diminish monetary pressure, and set out open doors for future ventures.

4. Contributing for What's to come:

Savvy money management is a propensity that stretches out past saving. People focused on monetary achievement figure out the significance of effective money management to develop abundance. They instruct themselves about various venture vehicles, broaden their portfolios, and take a drawn out point of view, permitting their speculations to intensify over the long run.

5. Keeping away from Motivation Buys:

The propensity for keeping away from motivation buys is pivotal for monetary achievement. People who oppose the charm of moment satisfaction and go with insightful spending choices are better situated to remain on financial plan and accomplish their monetary objectives.

6. Routinely Checking on and Changing Monetary Objectives:

Monetary achievement requires progressing reflection and change of monetary objectives. Laying out a propensity for routinely checking on and, if fundamental, changing monetary goals guarantees arrangement with changing conditions and needs. This versatile methodology adds to a strong monetary arrangement.

7. Overseeing and Paying off Past commitments:

Effective monetary people effectively oversee and pursue paying off past commitments. They focus on taking care of exorbitant interest obligations, try not to aggregate superfluous liabilities, and use obligation decisively when it lines up with their generally monetary arrangement.

8. Constant Finding out about Individual accounting:

Monetary achievement is frequently connected to monetary education. Developing a propensity for nonstop finding out about individual budget engages people to go with informed choices. This incorporates remaining informed about monetary patterns, charge suggestions, and changes in monetary guidelines.

9. Arranging and Looking for Worth:

Effective people foster a propensity for looking for esteem in their monetary exchanges. This incorporates haggling for more ideal arrangements, looking at costs, and being aware of the general offer in both regular costs and critical monetary responsibilities.

10. Laying out an Everyday practice for Monetary Registrations:
Normal monetary registrations structure a propensity that guarantees people stay associated with their monetary objectives. This routine incorporates surveying progress, distinguishing regions for development, and celebrating monetary achievements.

Taking everything into account, monetary propensities are the structure blocks of accomplishment. By integrating these propensities into day to day existence, people can make a strong and prosperous monetary future. Achievement isn't exclusively about the size of monetary choices however is molded by the total effect of predictable, positive monetary ways of behaving.

Section 9

Exploring Monetary Difficulties:

Monetary difficulties are an inescapable part of life, and the capacity to explore them really is significant for long-term monetary prosperity. Whether it's startling costs, employment misfortune, monetary slumps, or individual difficulties, how people answer these difficulties frequently determines their monetary flexibility. Here are key procedures for exploring monetary difficulties:

1. Backup stash as a wellbeing net:
Constructing and keeping a backup stash is a primary system for confronting unforeseen monetary difficulties. This asset fills in as a monetary wellbeing net, giving the liquidity expected to cover prompt costs without depending on exorbitant interest obligations.

2. Assess and Focus on Costs:
While confronting monetary difficulties, it's fundamental to assess and focus on costs. Recognise fundamental and insignificant spending, briefly scaling back optional costs while guaranteeing urgent requirements are met. Making a reexamined financial plan during testing times really oversees assets.

3. Correspondence and Discussion:
In the midst of monetary trouble, open correspondence becomes principal. Whether it's haggling with loan bosses, property managers, or specialist co-ops, making sense of the circumstances and looking for transitory help or changed terms can give you space to breathe while managing difficulties.

4. Looking for Proficient Guidance:
Monetary difficulties might warrant looking for guidance from monetary experts. Talking with monetary guides, bookkeepers, or obligation advocates can provide important experiences and techniques to address explicit difficulties. Proficient direction can assist people with settling on informed choices aligned with their monetary objectives.

5. Versatility and adaptability:

Monetary difficulties frequently require versatility and adaptability in one's methodology. This might include investigating elective revenue sources, taking into account vocation changes, or changing speculation systems. Being available to turn because of changing conditions is a vital part of exploring difficulties effectively.

6. Utilising Government Help and Projects:
During seasons of financial vulnerability or individual difficulty, government help projects can offer urgent help. Understanding and getting access to accessible assets, for example, joblessness advantages or help for lodging, can assist people with enduring monetary tempests all the more.

7. Protecting Mental and Close-to-Home Prosperity:
Monetary difficulties can negatively affect mental and profound prosperity. It's fundamental to focus on taking care of oneself and look for help when required. Keeping a positive outlook, setting practical assumptions, and perceiving that difficulties are brief can add to close-to-home strength during difficult stretches.

8. Vital Utilisation of Credit and Obligations:
While it's by and large fitting to limit dependence on layaway during testing times, key utilisation of credit or advances might be fundamental. Understanding the terms and ramifications of acquiring and utilising credit dependably can assist people with overseeing prompt necessities without compounding long-term monetary difficulties.

9. Persistent Acquiring and Expertise Advancement:
Confronting monetary difficulties frequently presents a chance for individual and expert development. Constant mastery and ability improvement, whether to upgrade employability or investigate new pay-producing roads, can add to long-haul monetary flexibility.

10. Keeping up with the Long-Hour Point of View:
Exploring monetary difficulties isn't just about prompt arrangements; additionally, it's about keeping a drawn-out viewpoint. Perceiving that difficulties are important for a bigger monetary excursion and effectively making progress towards long-haul monetary objectives can give a feeling of inspiration and direction.

All in all, exploring monetary difficulties requires a blend of proactive monetary preparation, versatility, and a strong mentality. By utilising these methodologies, people might weather hardships at any point as well as position themselves for long-haul money.

Conclusion:

In the unpredictable embroidery of individual budgets, the excursion towards monetary prosperity is set apart by smart choices, trained propensities, and a tough outlook. As we consider the standards framed in "How to Open Riches: Disclosing the Key to Monetary Overflow," obviously opening abundance is certainly not a particular objective yet a constant and deliberate pursuit.

The significance of defining clear monetary objectives couldn't possibly be more significant. This fundamental step shapes the direction of the whole monetary excursion. By articulating yearnings and laying out a deliberate association with cash, people set up a way that lines up with their interesting dreams and desires.

Building a strong monetary establishment arises as a foundation for progress. From fastidious planning and reasonable spending to the foundation of crisis reserves, a hearty monetary establishment gives strength even with vulnerabilities and lays the foundation for future development.

Savings arise as a monetary propensity as well as a strong device with extensive impacts. The demonstration of saving reaches beyond gathering reserves; it encourages discipline, makes monetary pads, and changes goals into unmistakable real factors. Through the force of saving, people develop a mentality of overflow, perceiving the potential for development and flourishing.

Savvy effective financial planning unfolds as a workmanship, requiring informed direction, enhancement, and a relentless obligation to long-term objectives. By embracing expanded techniques and remaining receptive to monetary patterns, people position themselves to seize the valuable open doors introduced by unique monetary business sectors.

Enhancement methodologies act as a safeguard against the unusualness of monetary business sectors. The conscious assignment of assets across various resources and areas mitigates chance and improves the versatility of venture portfolios. Through essential broadening, people invigorate their monetary positions, providing support against market instability.

Remaining informed about financial patterns is a proactive and enabling practice. In a period of interconnected worldwide economies, understanding the powers that shape monetary scenes is vital. Equipped with information, people pursue informed choices, explore difficulties, and profit from valuable open doors in an always-developing financial climate.

Developing an overflow outlook rises above monetary standards, turning into a directing way of thinking forever. It includes embracing appreciation, joint effort, and confidence in boundless potential outcomes. This attitude shapes monetary choices as well as impacts general prosperity by encouraging strength notwithstanding challenges and commending triumphs of all shapes and sizes.

Monetary propensities for progress highlight the groundbreaking effect of everyday ways of behaving. From planning and saving to managing money carefully and staying away from hasty choices, these propensities structure the texture of monetary achievement. Through predictable, positive monetary ways of behaving, people explore difficulties really as well as make an establishment for getting through success.

As we investigate the procedures for exploring difficulties, it becomes apparent that misfortunes are not barricades but rather potential open doors for development. From building crisis assets to arranging and looking for esteem, the capacity to adjust, learn, and continue on recognises the people who arise more grounded from monetary difficulties.

All in all, the excursion to open abundance is a dynamic and deliberate campaign. It is an excursion set apart by flexibility, ceaseless learning, and a guarantee of monetary prosperity. As people apply the standards examined in "How to Open Riches: Uncovering the Key to Monetary Overflow," they explore the intricacies of individual accounting as well as set out on an extraordinary mission towards a day-to-day existence wealthy in overflow, satisfaction, and perseverance through thriving.